NIGHTINGALE CONANT

# Table of Contents

# INTRODUCTION

## A SUCCESS SYSTEM FOR THE 21ST CENTURY

In 1956, Earl Nightingale wrote and recorded a message that he called *The Strangest Secret*. In a short period of time, without advertising or marketing, more than a million copies had been sold. In fact, *The Strangest Secret* earned a gold record—the only one ever achieved for the spoken word.

One of the people who heard *The Strangest Secret* was Lloyd Conant, the owner of a Chicago-based printing and direct response company. Lloyd contacted Earl and the two became fast friends. Their common bond? Their shared values of success.

In 1960, Earl Nightingale and Lloyd Conant formed the Nightingale-Conant corporation so that they could share those values with the world. They started with the now-classic success program *Lead The Field*. It became a best seller as well, touching the lives of more than a million people.

Since then, Nightingale-Conant has featured the wisdom and success principles of hundreds of individuals who are at the top of virtually every industry.

After 50 years of teaching success, Nightingale Learning Systems has gathered together the common bonds and shared values of those individuals who occupy the rarest positions in their industries—the top 2 percent.

With *The Top 2%*, our intention is to provide the latest research on what it takes to reach the top in the 21st Century—the road map for the next generation of achievers–starting with you.

Simple Truths is truly honored to be involved in bringing this great content to life.

All the best,

Founder, Simple Truths

"ENTHUSIASM IS THE YEAST THAT MAKES YOUR HOPES SHINE TO THE STARS. ENTHUSIASM IS THE SPARKLE IN YOUR EYES, THE SWING IN YOUR GAIT. THE GRIP OF YOUR HAND, THE IRRESISTIBLE SURGE OF WILL AND ENERGY TO EXECUTE YOUR IDEAS."

HENRY FORD

# The Top 2 Percent

You might be wondering, "Why the 2 percent? Most leaders and success experts only look at the top 5 percent. What's so special about the 2 PERCENT?"

Even when you're not talking about money, it's still better to be in the top 2 percent than the top 5 percent. Wouldn't you rather be in the top 2 percent of healthy people? The top 2 percent of happy people? Have relationships that are better than 98 percent of everyone else?

The fact is, the days when being in the top 5 percent was good enough are gone. We live in a global village with, frankly, a bigger pool of talented motivated people who are competing against you. When you apply these ideas and techniques, you'll be poised to be in the top 2 percent of any area in which you choose to succeed.

Have you ever wondered what the superstars of success do on a daily basis? *The Top 2%* will help you discover not only the tips, techniques, and actions that will lead you to the STARS, but also the mindset. For the people who live among the stars do so because every thought, every word, and every action comes from their dreams. George Bernard Shaw said, "You see things and you say, 'Why?' But I dream things that never were and I say, '**Why not?**'"

**Dream things that never were! Dream them into existence! All things are possible for those who believe.**

The fact is, the top 2 percent set the trends in every industry. They set the trends by imagining and dreaming things that didn't exist and then doing what it took to make it happen. Whether you're in business, entertainment, sports, politics or some other industry, if you're in the top 2 percent, you have the power and influence to make things happen.

At Nightingale Learning Systems, we spent months researching through our library and identified 17 principles of success that were common among all of our top authors. We then arranged the 17 principles into a model that is represented by the shape of a star.

## Each of the points of the star represents one area of success:

**S** - Sense of Purpose

**T** - Traits

**A** - Attitudes

**R** - Rapport with Others

**S** - Skills

Are you ready to rocket to the STARS? Your dreams are like the stars you see in the night sky. You may never touch them, but if you follow them, they will lead you to your destiny.

# STARS

## The Top Quality of the Top 2 Percent:
## An Overarching **SENSE OF PURPOSE**

There is one quality that runs through all 17 principles. It's *An Overarching Sense of Purpose*. It's the thing that makes you reach higher and higher.

As Ken Blanchard put it, "Purpose is something bigger. It is the picture you have of yourself—the kind of person you want to be or the kind of life you want to lead."

In a book called *Recovering the Soul*, Dr. Larry Darcy said that human beings are the only living species that have achieved the dubious distinction of dying or having a stroke or heart attack on a certain day.  Did you know that more heart attacks take place in this country on Monday morning between 8:00 and 9:00 a.m. than any other time of the day or week?

Eighty-five percent of the American public, according to recent studies, are going to jobs that they hate or that do not challenge them. Think about it this way. When you go to a job that isn't part of an overarching sense of purpose, it's like going to a movie where you've already seen the end. You know what the outcome is going to be. You can't get excited about going through that movie all over again. Contrast this where you're going to a job and you have a strong sense that what you do matters. It doesn't even have to be brain surgery. You could be the guy that puts the paper clips inside the paper clip box. But if you have a sense of purpose and meaning about it, you're not going to be the one dropping dead of a heart attack on Monday morning.

### *Your life is worth finding out what it is you are supposed to do.*

How much time do you spend working on you? How much time do you spend every day working on your dream? In the last 90 days, how many books have you read? In the last year, what new skill or knowledge have you acquired? What kind of investment have you made in you?

When you are part of the top 2 percent, you are working on yourself so that you can live your life with the greatest sense of purpose possible.

Having an overarching sense of purpose may be key to getting into the top 2 percent of your field, but how do you do it? The way to identify your overarching sense of purpose is to think about what things bother you the most.

For example, I know a woman who is a health coach. She says that it drives her nuts when she goes to the grocery store and sees people who are clearly unhealthy filling their carts with junk food. It makes her so mad! It was this anger that led her to become a health coach and to start helping people to see the connection between what they eat and the diseases they have. She went back to school, learned about physiology and nutrition and became a health coach because she was bothered by what she saw at the grocery store.

Think about what problems in life bother you the most. Perhaps it's animal rights or something to do with politics. Whatever it is, you can tell by the emotional charge you get by talking about it.

Does this mean you need to go and change your career? No, not at all. If you're passionate about animal rights, you don't need to become a veterinarian. Maybe you can write articles. Maybe you can volunteer at a shelter. Maybe you should become a vegetarian. You see, the overarching sense of purpose is what makes you **REACH** higher.

By finding your overarching sense of purpose and focusing on it, you'll find yourself with a drive and a passion you never felt before! As Dostoyevsky put it, **"The secret of a man's being is not only to live, but to have something to live for."**

# Find out what you're living for, and you'll be on your way to the STARS.

SENSE OF PURPOSE

THE TOP 2%

# STARS

## TRAITS: *Passion*
## The High Octane Performance Fuel

Traits refer to the letter *T* in our STARS model and are the "personality traits" that the STARS have in common. These aren't things you're born with—they are personality traits that can be LEARNED.

As Virginia Voeks put it, "We learn only what we do. And what we do, we become. Live, therefore, in the ways you desire to have as part of your personality. Practice being the person you wish to become."

The four personality traits that the STARS have in common are something that you can absolutely learn to develop too!

The first trait is *Passion*. It's the fuel that drives you to the STARS. As Nightingale Conant author Larry Winget puts it, "Excellence is what moves you to the top. And hard work doing the right things is what makes you excellent. To tell people that passion is the key to success does those folks a great disservice. Because somewhere down the road, they will discover that no one cares or shares their passion. They will find out that while they are passionate, they haven't done the work to be really good, they know nothing about selling or marketing, leadership, management, finance, their competition, serving customers or all the other facets of a successful life or business. All they have is their passion. Try cashing that at the bank."

This quote gets to the heart of the message. Passion is the FUEL that will drive you to become excellent. If you have a passionate feeling, it's not enough. You have to translate that passionate feeling into directed, focused action. But taking actions without the fuel of passion doesn't work either.

The STARS who are in the top 2 percent of their fields are there because they FEEL passion and that passion has fueled them to become excellent.

# How can you develop a passion for something?

# How can you develop high octane performance fuel

# for ANY AREA you want?

TRAITS

# HERE ARE THREE STEPS.

 **Fill up the tank**

To increase your level of passion about something, fill up your tank! Learn as much as you can. Of course, it's going to be easier if it's a topic you're naturally interested in. But you can develop a passion for absolutely anything if you learn enough about it.

 **Use high quality fuel**

We live in an information age. No matter what topic you're thinking about, there are hundreds of sources out there with information. Make sure you are using high quality sources for your information. Be discerning. There is a huge difference between reading a tabloid newspaper and a textbook. Look to people who are in the top 2 percent of the field you're studying and learn from them. Those are going to be the best sources of information.

 **Drive all over town**

Once you've filled up your tank with high quality fuel, take it all over town! Get excited about sharing your ideas with other people. It's not about being pushy, it's about having so much passion and excitement about your subject that you WANT to tell people about it.

How can you run all over town with your idea? Can you get some business cards printed up? Can you go to shows? Join a club? Build a network? How can you get other people passionate about your passion? One of the reasons that STARS are STARS is because not only do they have passion themselves, but they make YOU feel passionate too.

Fill up the tank

Use high quality fuel

Drive all over town

TRAITS

# TRAITS: *An Innovative Spirit*

The second trait that is common among the STARS is an *innovative or an entrepreneurial spirit.*

Here's an example from *Heart at Work* by Petey Parker:

A cab driver taught me a million-dollar lesson in customer satisfaction and expectation. Motivational speakers charge thousands of dollars to impart his kind of training to corporate executives and staff. It cost me a $12 taxi ride.

I had flown into Dallas for the sole purpose of calling on a client. A spotless cab pulled up. The driver rushed to open the passenger door for me and made sure I was comfortably seated before he closed the door. As he got in the driver's seat, he mentioned that the neatly folded *Wall Street Journal* next to me was for my use. He then showed me several tapes and asked me what type of music I would enjoy. I could not believe the service I was receiving! I took the opportunity to say, "Obviously you take great pride in your work. You must have a story to tell."

"You bet," he replied, "I used to be in corporate America. But I got tired of thinking my best would never be good enough. I decided to find my niche in life where I could feel proud of being the best I could be. I knew I would never be a rocket scientist, but I love driving cars, being of service and feeling like I have done a full day's work and done it well. I evaluated my personal assets and... wham! I became a cab driver. One thing I know for sure, to be good in my business I could simply just meet the expectations of my passengers. But, to be GREAT in my business, I have to EXCEED the customer's expectations! I like both the sound and the return of being 'great' better than just getting by on 'average.'"

Did I tip him big time? You bet! Corporate America's loss is the traveling folk's friend!

Now think about that. Wouldn't you say that the taxi driver is in the top 2 percent of all taxi drivers? You see, we're not necessarily talking about leaving your job or starting your own company. It might just mean thinking a little differently about what you do every day.

Regardless of whether you are an entrepreneur, you can LEARN to have an entrepreneurial or innovative spirit— the O.W.L Method, which stands for *Own, Win, Leverage.*

# Using the O.W.L Method

You have to have an attitude of **O**WN*ership* over your work, you have to have a **WIN**ning attitude of perseverance, and you have to *LEVERAGE* what you've got into something more. What does this mean?

# Own

The attitude of the cab driver is the perfect example of an attitude of *OWN*ing your work. It doesn't matter if you're the CEO of a company, if you have a small business you're running out of your garage, or if you work at a retail establishment; it's about having a sense of pride and ownership in what you do. Peter Drucker made an astute observation when he said, "The purpose of a business is to create a customer." And those who are in the top 2 percent understand that.

*The essence of the **OWN** part of the **O.W.L.** method is to develop the desire to be the **VERY BEST** at whatever you're doing.*

# Win

The second element of the O.W.L. method of entrepreneurship and innovation is *Win*, illustrated by this story about George Washington from Adam Kahn:

On his first military campaign, George Washington made a terrible mistake. The American colonies had not yet rebelled—that was 20 years down the road. Washington was working for Britain, which was in a "cold war" with France. One day Washington and his troops spotted a party of French camping in their territory, and attacked them, killing ten men and capturing the rest.

You **CAN** rewrite the past so that you're the winner of your life's story.

TRAITS

He shot first and asked questions later. He found out it was a diplomatic party, and one of the men he killed was an important French ambassador. Washington had made a big mistake. The two major military powers of that time ended their cold war and entered a hot war.

What Washington could have told himself was, "I am destined for failure." His father died young; his mother was a nag. Compared to his contemporaries, he was poor. Killing the French ambassador could have been a final straw. He might have concluded that he wasn't cut out for military work and given up, climbed inside a bottle and we might never have heard of him.

Here's another possibility: He could have thought he was destined to make his mark in the world, and that his mistake was the most important lesson he was ever to learn. "Divine Providence," he could have told himself, "is preparing me for a great task. I must learn all I can from this mistake for it may affect the future of the world."

Do you think he would feel differently about the circumstances of his life with this story? Of course he would. Same circumstances, different story. But the heroic story would make him learn important military lessons from his mistake and it would help him persist and endure hardships that would collapse a weaker person. The story would give him strength.

To WIN you have to be persistent. You have to know that you're going to make it into that top 2 percent and if something happens that looks like a problem, rewrite it into a powerful story that supports your success.

## You CAN rewrite the past so that you're the winner of your life's story.

# Leverage

The final element of the O.W.L. method is *Leverage.* By leverage we mean taking what you've got and using it to make more. Peter Drucker described it this way, "The entrepreneur always searches for change, responds to it, and exploits it as an opportunity."

The Leverage component of the Own, Win, Leverage model is about taking whatever life gives you, whether it's good or bad, and making it into something better. It's about seeing a problem or a change, finding a solution, and running with it.

# TO RECAP THE O.W.L. METHOD:

⭐ Take **OWN**ership of your work;

⭐ Have a **WIN**ning attitude regardless of what happens to you;

⭐ **L**EVERAGE the events of your life into something greater.

THE TOP 2%

# SHEDDING YOUR SELF-IMPOSTER

The STARS understand that in order for others to see us as valuable, we first have to value ourselves. Norman Vincent Peale said, "People become really quite remarkable when they start thinking that they can do things. When they believe in themselves they have the first secret of success."

Self-image isn't based on what's in reality. It's based on your BELIEFS about yourself. In order to change your self-image, you have to change your beliefs about yourself.

So, how can you use this concept of self-image and self-regard to become one of the STARS?  Here is a story from Brian Cavanaugh in his book, *The Sower's Seeds*.

It's about Sir Edmund Hillary, the first man to climb Mount Everest. On May 29, 1953 he scaled the highest mountain then known to man–29,000 feet straight up. He was knighted for his efforts.

However, until we read his book, *High Adventure*, we don't understand that Hillary had to grow into this success.

You see, in 1952 he attempted to climb Mount Everest, but failed. A few weeks later a group in England asked him to address its members.

Hillary walked on stage to a thunderous applause. The audience was recognizing an attempt at greatness, but Edmund Hillary saw himself as a failure. He moved away from the microphone and walked to the edge of the platform.

He made a fist and pointed at a picture of the mountain. He said in a loud voice, "Mount Everest, you beat me the first time, but I'll beat you the next time because you've grown all you are going to grow... but I'm still growing!"

Are you still growing? Are you presenting yourself with opportunities that challenge yourself to grow? It's not always about "feeling good about yourself." No. In fact,

in order to become one of the highest paid and highest profile people in your industry, you're going to have to grow. You're going to have to try new things and you're going to fail. But as long as you keep getting back up again and reaching for new heights, you WILL find yourself among the STARS.

"BELIEF IN ONESELF IS ONE OF THE MOST IMPORTANT BRICKS IN BUILDING ANY SUCCESSFUL VENTURE."

LYNDA M. CHILD

**TRAITS**

## TRAITS: *High Energy and Enthusiasm*

The last trait of the highest paid, highest profile people in ANY industry is high energy and enthusiasm.

Here's a whimsical poem that captures the trait:

# I Resign

*I am hereby officially tendering my resignation as an adult.*
*I have decided I would like to accept the responsibilities of an 8-year-old again.*
*I want to go to McDonalds and think that it's a four-star restaurant.*
*I want to sail sticks across a fresh mud puddle and make ripples with rocks.*
*I want to think M&Ms are better than money because you can eat them.*
*I want to lie under a big oak tree and run a lemonade stand with my friends on a hot summer day.*
*I want to return to a time when life was simple.*

*When all you knew were colors, multiplication tables, and nursery rhymes, but that didn't bother you, because you didn't know what you didn't know and you didn't care.*

*All you knew was to be happy because you were blissfully unaware of all the things that should make you worried or upset.*

*I want to think the world is fair. That everyone is honest and good.*

*I want to believe that anything is possible.*

*I want to be oblivious to the complexities of life and be overly excited by the little things again.*

*I want to live simple again.*

*I don't want my day to consist of computer crashes, mountains of paperwork, depressing news, how to survive more days in the month than there is money in the bank, doctor bills, gossip, illness, and loss of loved ones.*

*I want to believe in the power of smiles, hugs, a kind word, truth, justice, peace, dreams, the imagination, mankind, and making angels in the snow.*

TRAITS

*So… here's my checkbook and my car keys, my credit cards and all my responsibility.*

*I am officially resigning from adulthood. And if you want to discuss this further, you'll have to catch me first, 'cause, "Tag! You're it."* ~ Author Unknown

How perfectly does that poem capture the essence of enthusiasm? Kids have unbridled energy and passion. But, for most people, that eventually changes. They discover the snooze button on their alarms. Instead of jumping out of bed to greet the day, they roll over for ten more minutes of sleep. Instead of playing until their eyelids droop, most people plop in front of the television, sitting there until they doze off.

> *What happened? More importantly, does it happen to everyone?*

The top 2 percent of any industry DON'T lose their enthusiasm and energy. Or, if they lose it, they get it back and that's what gets them to the top.

How can YOU develop the ability to be high energy and have enthusiasm like those in the top 2 percent? The Always On™ Process will help you to skyrocket your physical, mental, and spiritual energy. Here's how it works.

TRAITS

Every day, you need to replenish your energy in each of three areas: *Physical Energy, Mental Energy, and Spiritual Energy.* Decide what times of day you need to boost which type of energy.

Then, add in some activities that boost your energy in that particular area during the time when you feel your energy lagging.

# "PASSION IS ENERGY. FEEL THE POWER THAT COMES FROM FOCUSING ON WHAT EXCITES YOU."

**OPRAH WINFREY**

TRAITS

## REPLENISH YOUR ENERGY

# In the morning

✤ For physical energy, eat breakfast and exercise in the morning.

✤ For mental energy, you might do a mental "PhotoShopping" exercise—where you create a mental image of yourself as an energetic, enthusiastic person and then see that person stepping into the image of the current you, replacing your low energy self with a high energy version of you.

✤ For a spiritual boost in the morning, go outside and have your morning coffee or tea in the garden or on your patio.

# In the afternoon

✣ Listen to some uplifting motivational music.

✣ Have some fruit and protein or go for a little walk and drink some water.

✣ And if your mental energy is starting to dip, close your eyes and take a five-minute mental vacation.

# In the evening

✤ Try a Happiness Hour— a period of time after you get home from work where you sit down and reconnect with the people you love.

By consciously managing your energy in terms of physical energy, mental energy, and spiritual energy, you'll be able to make the most of each day. You'll be energized and enthusiastic about your life, which is a key trait of those who are in the top 2 percent.

Walter Chrysler put it this way, "…Enthusiasm is at the bottom of all progress. With it, there is accomplishment. Without it, there are only alibis."

*Sit down and reconnect with the people you love.*

TRAITS

THE TOP 2%

# STARS

## ATTITUDES: *Healthy Habits*

The next point on the STARS model is **Attitudes**. There are four attitudes that people who are the highest paid, highest profile people in their industries have in common. The first one is *healthy habits*.

It's about listening to your body and developing habits for health that work with YOUR life and YOUR body. It's about valuing your body as the vehicle that gets you to your goals. Your body is, in essence, the rocket ship that will get you to the STARS. And like any NASA engineer will tell you, you've got to maintain that rocket so that it will perform at its best.

For the people who are in the top 2 percent, healthy habits are like a reflex. For them, making healthy choices is as automatic as breathing or lifting their hand from a hot stove. They don't have to "try" to be healthy. They just are.

So how can you do that? How can you use your body as a vehicle that will propel you to the top 2 percent of your field? You have to think about your health in terms of your whole LIFE instead of how you look in a bathing suit or how you perform in sports. It's thinking about health as a HABIT instead of a destination. That's an important distinction.

It's not something that you do for six weeks or six months until you hit a goal and then you stop. The people who are the highest paid, highest profile people in their industries have made health a HABIT in their daily life.

ATTITUDES

Customize a program that works for YOU and your particular situation. No matter how fit or healthy you are, you've got to work on it every day. It's about implementing healthy habits that will fuel your success, allowing you to reach the STARS.

## "TO KEEP THE BODY IN GOOD HEALTH IS A DUTY...OTHERWISE WE SHALL NOT BE ABLE TO KEEP OUR MIND STRONG AND CLEAR."

**BUDDHA**

# ATTITUDES: *Continual Learning*

The second attitude among the highest paid, highest profile people in any industry is an *attitude of continual learning*. What have YOU learned lately?

Now, you might be thinking, "I don't have time to be continually learning new things. Sure, I'd love to learn how to windsurf. But I'm too busy doing my J.O.B. and all the other things I need to get done in a day."

What are some of the excuses we tell ourselves that keep us from being a continual learner? Not enough time is a big one. The "not enough time" excuse is really just a matter of priorities. It's a matter of understanding the benefits of continual learning and then looking for opportunities to learn something new. We're talking about an attitude that every day brings new learning and being open to what life has to teach us.

Brian Tracy said, "Commit yourself to lifelong learning. The most valuable asset you'll ever have is your mind and what you put into it."

You don't ever need to step foot in a classroom to develop an attitude of continual learning. Hands-on learning and observation are among the most powerful tools for learning.

To become a lifelong learner, you need to follow what we call The EVO Learning System. It covers the three main areas of learning— formal education; things you learn just for fun, like a hobby or a mental vacation from your life; and things that are related to your work or career.

ATTITUDES

**So EVO learning stands for
E: Education, V: Vacation,
and O: Occupation.**

# Education

You can have the same people, twins even. One becomes a doctor and one drops out of high school. They could be equally wonderful people, great parents, have the same talents and personality. But the one who has more formal education will be earning almost $104,000 more than the other one! The more formal education you have, the more financially rewarded you will be.

ATTITUDES

# Vacation

These are the kinds of activities that you do that let you leave your work or schooling behind. It's a hobby or an avocation that you do to relieve stress or increase pleasure.

# Occupation

This is learning you do to further your career, not necessarily additional training or certifications, although that's fine. It's an attitude of openness. It's about not becoming so engrained in your work that you lose sight of creative or new ways of doing things or of being.

Whether you're a solo-preneur, a freelance writer, a small business owner, a therapist, or are inside a corporation, you can use a learning technique we developed called The Flexback Technique, which is based on the work of Nightingale Conant author Marshall Goldsmith.  Marshall was a pioneer of a 360-degree feedback technique used within corporations to help leaders at all levels of management learn how to use feedback from their bosses, peers and direct reports.

ATTITUDES

To use the Flexback technique, you want to identify the key stakeholders in your work. These are people who have an interest in your business. Of course customers come to mind. But also think about anyone who is related to your work. So, if you're an artist, you might think of the suppliers that you use for your raw materials. If you have any employees, they are stakeholders. If you have a boss, that person would be a stakeholder.

Approach your stakeholders and ask their opinions about how you're doing. Depending on the dynamics of your work situation, you could do it face to face or through a survey. Every person you work with has something that he or she can teach you. If you open yourself up to the message, you will be a much richer person, both professionally and personally.

Asking the questions is only the first half of the FlexBack Technique. One of the things Marshall Goldsmith teaches leaders is to set a specific date for follow-up. In other words, contact the person again to let them know what the impact of his or her feedback was. You can use the FlexBack technique in your personal life too.

Whether you're getting a formal education, vacating from your life in the form of a hobby, or you're learning in your occupation, an EVO Learner is someone who is always growing.

# ATTITUDES: *Be Strategically Content*

The third attitude in our STARS model is being *Strategically Content*. Which should you be focusing on— goals for the future or being happy in the here and now?

That is the age-old question in the field of personal development. Why would you want to change your life if you're happy with it? How can you balance out the ideas of achieving goals and being happy now? It seems like a paradox, doesn't it?

People are used to being told to be "content." But, paradoxically, successful people are never totally content—in many ways it is discontent with their current circumstance that drives them to achieve. And, no matter how much these folks have achieved, they're never really content to rest on their laurels. They're always looking for the next challenge. But, that doesn't mean that they are unhappy people.

The top 2 percent of achievers are "strategic" about what they choose to be content about. They realize that there are certain situations, relationships and circumstances where contentment is a virtue (such as playing with your children, tending to a sick parent, listening to your spouse, et cetera.) However, they also realize that there are areas where total contentment is a vice (such as being totally content to stay in a dead-end job that offers no growth or challenge—where you just punch the clock day after day and "mail it in").

Benjamin Franklin summed up the idea of being strategically content perfectly when he said, "Content makes poor men rich; discontent makes rich men poor."

You have to be strategic about what you're content with.

Are you waiting to be happy? Have you said to yourself, "I'll be so happy when I reach my goal weight?" "Yeah, I'd be happy if I had a million dollars and could quit this

ATTITUDES

lousy job." Or maybe, "I'll be happy when I buy that car, a house, get my degree, get married, have children…" When does it stop? Can you imagine waiting until your sixties or seventies to "be happy?" Looking back on your life and feeling like you'd wasted it because you were waiting for a future time to be happy?

Don't do that! Being happy in the present moment doesn't mean that you don't have goals. In fact, being happy in the present moment is a PREREQUISITE for achieving your goals.  As one of our personal coaches at Nightingale Conant tells clients, "The seeds of your future happiness are present in your life today. It's up to you to shower them with attention so that they grow."

So, how can you become Strategically Content? *The Ready, Set, Let Go* process covers the three elements of being Strategically Content:

✵ Get *Ready*—establish a goal and plan for it.

✵ Get *Set*—take the actions necessary to achieve the goal.

✵ Let *Go*— detach from the outcome. This last step is often the hardest step for a lot of people, but it's also the most important part.

It's like when you plant a garden. You get ready by deciding which plants to plant, getting the soil and seeds and digging up the area. Then, you get set. You actually plant the seeds into the ground and water them regularly. But, once this is done, you have to let go. You can't go out there and dig up the seed every day saying, "Is it a strawberry yet?" No, you have to get ready, get set, and then LET IT GO. Dreams and goals, like seeds, grow in their own time. Might as well be happy and enjoy yourself while they're growing.

ATTITUDES

Flugelhorn jazz player John DePaola says it this way, "Slow down and everything you are chasing will come around and catch you."

And the best part is, while you're rising to the STARS and becoming one of the highest paid, highest profile people in your industry, you'll gain one thing that money can't buy—*HAPPINESS*.

# "HAPPINESS IS NOT SOMETHING YOU POSTPONE FOR THE FUTURE; IT IS SOMETHING YOU DESIGN FOR THE PRESENT."

**JIM ROHN**

ATTITUDES

# ATTITUDES: *Self-Discipline*

Usually when you hear the words "self-discipline" you think of "making yourself do what you should do." We're going to look at self-discipline as an ATTITUDE rather than a set of behaviors. Here's a story that illustrates the difference.

A successful real estate agent was approached by a younger agent who worked at a competing firm. The younger agent said, "I'm sure you won't want to do this, but is there any way we could meet for coffee and you could share with me what it is that you do that makes you so successful?" The successful agent agreed without hesitation. They sat for two hours at a local coffee house and the successful agent told his young competitor the many disciplines that he regularly used to succeed so well. As they were leaving, the younger agent said, "Why did you agree to do this? Aren't you afraid that I'll use all your suggestions and take away your business?" To which the successful agent replied, "I'm not worried about that at all. Very few people are willing to do what I do to be successful."

Can you see the difference? The successful agent had an ATTITUDE of self-discipline, and the younger agent wanted to know the ACTIONS of self-discipline.

A person with self-discipline is a person who has an attitude of learning in his or her field of study. That's what self-discipline is! Being a disciple in your field.

When you define self-discipline that way, you go from feeling like, "Ugh, I have to have more willpower so that I can make myself do what I need to do," to feeling like, "What can I learn today that will make me more successful in my field?"

As musician David Campbell said, "Discipline is remembering what you want."

ATTITUDES

To access that inner disciple—the one who *wants* to do what he or she needs to do, follow our Mental Alignment Process, or M.A.P. for short. The M.A.P. process can take you from where you are now to where you want to be and help keep you motivated on course even when obstacles arise.

## Here are the elements of the M.A.P. process:

Choosing your destination
Deciding when to start
Determining your route
Preparing for the journey
Embarking on the journey
Identifying obstacles and roadblocks
Deciding whether to turn back or press on
Choosing another path
Staying the course
Celebrating your arrival

Whenever you find your motivation for the journey lagging, go back to this process and see where you are.

Earl Nightingale said, "All you need is the plan, the road map, and the courage to press on to your destination."

The M.A.P. Process can be the tool that helps you stay mentally aligned with your goals. It can help you stay focused on having an attitude of learning, asking, "What needs to change so that I can reach this goal?" It's about staying the course until you become one of the STARS.

ATTITUDES

"A GOAL WITHOUT A PLAN IS JUST A WISH."

ANTOINE DE SAINT-EXUPERY

ATTITUDES

# STARS

## RAPPORT: *Being Legacy Minded*

The next point in our STARS model, the R, stands for *Rapport.* There are five Rapport qualities in our model: being *legacy minded, demonstrating effective communication, being service oriented, and having fulfilling relationships.*

The top 2 percent are always thinking about making an impact—about leaving their legacy. They're thinking about making changes that will last beyond their individual lives. They know that it's your relationships with other people and the impact that you have on them when you're alive that defines your legacy.

*Roger Ebert is a perfect example of these ideas:*

He began his career as a professional critic in 1967, writing for the *Chicago Sun-Times*. In 1975, he branched out into television with a weekly film review show. He and his first co-host, Gene Siskel, coined the phrase "two thumbs up" to indicate a movie that both critics liked. In 2002, Roger Ebert developed thyroid cancer and has had numerous surgeries in an attempt to save his life. During the surgeries, he lost his lower jaw and therefore his ability to speak. Now, he's required to use a computerized voice to speak the words that used to flow effortlessly from his mouth.

Roger Ebert has committed himself to leaving a new legacy —the perfection of computer voice technology. In the months that followed the loss of his voice, Roger Ebert grew frustrated as he explored different ways to communicate. Because he'd had a career on television, he had many, many hours of his natural voice on audio.

He sent them to a Scottish company, which developed a computerized speech program from the recordings of Ebert's own voice. While it does bear the most resemblance to his original voice, it still sounds stilted and unnatural. But Roger Ebert is committed to being the public face for those with speaking disabilities. He says, "Because of the digital revolution, I have a voice, and I do not need to scream."

Roger Ebert had thought his legacy was going to be in the area of movie reviews. Perhaps he thought his greatest contribution would be the "two thumbs up" concept. And he definitely was a significant influence in popular culture. But then he became ill and his ability to speak was taken away.

He may not be able to leave his legacy any more using words. But being legacy minded means staying open to the meaning of your life and thinking about the impact it will have on others, and the world at large.

Everyone leaves a legacy. Whether you're thinking about it or not, the people around you are watching how you live your life and are learning from it. Good or bad, your actions and words are defining how you are remembered. This is your Unintentional Legacy—the impact you are having on the people around you.

You also have an Intentional Legacy, one you INTEND to leave. It is defined by how others approach work and life as a result of having known you.

To leave a lasting legacy, you must first align the various parts of your mind with the legacy that you wish to leave.

The next step is to create your Legacy Letter—a formalized statement of the values, behaviors, and approaches to life that you wish those who you leave behind to carry on.

RAPPORT

You should revisit your Legacy Letter at least once a year to make sure that your Intentional Legacy is aligned with your Unintentional Legacy.

U.S. Senator Paul Tsongas captured the essence of a legacy beautifully when he said, "We are a continuum. Just as we reach back to our ancestors for our fundamental values, so we, as guardians of that legacy, must reach ahead to our children and their children. And we do so with a sense of sacredness in that reaching."

# RAPPORT: *Effective Communication*

## *The second quality in Rapport is Effective Communication.*

The essence of good communication is being able to understand the INTENT behind what someone says, not just the literal words.

In his book, *The Heart of Coaching*, Thomas Crane says, "Communication filters distort the clarity of a message the same way a prism or camera filter bends or distorts light. They affect how you say what you say and how I hear it…And as the group becomes larger, the potential for confusion and chaos rises exponentially, as each person's filters distorts group communication in unpredictable ways."

The highest paid, highest profile people in any field have learned how to masterfully navigate this complicated web of communication filters.

RAPPORT

How CAN you improve your *Advanced Communication Aptitude*? To help you understand better how the top 2 percent of their fields communicate, we developed the **A.C.A.** model:

# Ask

Listen for relevant information, taking into account any communication filters that the person might be operating with. Common ways to ask include the phrases:

"What's going on?"

"I'd really like to hear your input on this."

"Please let me know if you see it differently."

"Don't worry about hurting my feelings; I'd really like to know your thoughts."

Then you need to reflect back your understanding of the relevant information.

"Okay, so let me make sure I understand…"

It's important to make sure that your own filters aren't affecting the communication. These phrases and questions should be said with an attitude of openness.

If you feel that emotions are running high, take a break and come back to the conversation when you've evaluated your own filters.

RAPPORT

# Consider

Identify the communication style of the person you are communicating with. Then, using the person's communication style, you share all relevant information, including what you learned from the other person and what you're bringing to the conversation.

RAPPORT

# Act

This is a critical part of the conversation because a conversation is not the same thing as a decision. If you're not "on the same page" as they say, about what is going to come after the conversation, expectations can be violated later on. One person can think the conversation meant one thing and the other can think it meant something completely different.

To prevent this is, before you make a decision about what the next steps are, jointly decide how to decide.

Once this is done and the decisions have been made, it's important to clarify everyone's roles. You need to decide WHO does WHAT by WHEN and what it's going to look like when it's done.

The highest paid, highest profile people in every field know that having Advanced Communication Aptitude and using the A.C.A. model of communication in ALL situations is the cornerstone to success. It's not something they turn on and off. They take the time to effectively communicate with each and every person they deal with.

RAPPORT

# RAPPORT: *Be Service Oriented - The Service Paradox*

In *Lead the Field*, Earl Nightingale describes the importance of being service oriented this way:

"Working hard is not enough. Your rewards in life will always match the level of your service..."

Earl perfectly describes what we are calling the service paradox. The more you serve others, the more you receive in return. And, the more you receive, the more resources you have to share with others. The people who are the highest paid, highest profile people in any industry got that way because they understand the truth in what Earl Nightingale said. My rewards in life will be in exact proportion to my service.

# Here are 6 principles to the Service Paradox.

## Principle #1:

*The person you serve may not always appreciate it, or may come to take it for granted. But a reward will come to you from another source.*

# Principle #2:

*You have to seize the moments to serve when they happen, even if you're afraid.* Actress and comedienne Rosie O' Donnell tells a story about her son, who was 6 years old at the time of the September 11th attacks in New York. Shortly after the attacks, Rosie's son, Parker, insisted that she take him to a fire station, even though she feared he was too young to deal with all the pain there. But he said, "Mommy, I need to go." Eventually she took him there, and there were these shell-shocked firemen dressed in their formal blue uniforms on the way to yet another funeral and grieving for fifteen of their firehouse brothers who'd died in the attacks on the World Trade Center. Parker walked over to a very big fireman and tugged on his coat. The fireman stooped down and Parker said, "I'm sorry your friends died to save us. But they're with God now." Parker, the fireman and everyone else who had heard, started to cry. Rosie realized that while she that while she had wanted to protect her son, thinking it would be too much for him, he ended up serving them all in a way that none of them would ever forget.

## Principle #3:

*Your reward doesn't always come in the way you expect.*

## Principle #4:

*Serving and receiving are halves of a circle.* The more you focus on the little ways that you are blessed and the ways that you are receiving, the more you will receive. It's circular.

# Principle #5:

*You may never know the impact of your service.* United States Senator John McCain tells a story about a gift he received from a fellow prisoner when he was a prisoner of war in Vietnam. Senator McCain was imprisoned for five and a half years, and much of that time was spent in solitary confinement. McCain says:

"It was Christmas Eve, 1969. I was in pretty bad shape [physically and emotionally]. The prison guards began playing Dinah Shore singing, *'I'll be home for Christmas.'* As I lay there listening to that particular song, my spirits dropped to the lowest possible point. I wasn't sure I could survive another night, let alone ever return home for another Christmas with my family.

"It was then that I heard tapping on my wall. Despite strict rules against it, the POWs had devised a simple tapping code to communicate with each other by tapping on the walls.

"The cell on one side of me was empty, but in the other adjacent room was a guy named Ernie Brace. Ernie was a decorated former Marine who had flown more than 100 combat missions in the Korean War and then had volunteered as a civilian pilot in the Vietnam War.

"As soon as I heard the tapping I knew it was Ernie. I pressed my ear against the cold stone wall, and soon the message became very clear.

"We'll all be home for Christmas," Ernie tapped. "God Bless America."

"That simple message, in my darkest hour, strengthened my will to live."

Ernie didn't know whether or not John McCain could hear the tapping. He had no idea that it was the darkest hour of his life. But the gift he gave, not knowing whether or not it was even heard, is what helped John McCain survive solitary confinement and return to a life of service in the United States government.

**RAPPORT**

# Principle #6:

*Your service may be a small contribution, but it matters to someone.* In 2009, President Barack Obama gave a speech designed to inspire Americans to service. In the speech, he shared a well known story by Loren Eisley about a little boy on the beach. It goes like this:

An old man walking along the beach at dawn sees a young man picking up starfish and throwing them out to sea. "Why are you doing that?" the old man inquired. The young man explained that the starfish had been stranded on the beach by a receding tide and would soon die in the daytime sun. "But the beach goes on for miles," the old man said. "And there are so many! How can your effort make any difference?" The young man looked at the starfish in his hand and without hesitating threw it to safety in the sea. He looked up at the old man, smiled and said, "It will make a difference to that one."

We are all connected, and when we serve, we receive. No matter who you are or how much or little you have to give, being service oriented is about having an attitude of service and giving on a daily basis. It's not always about donating to something big. It's what you do EVERY DAY.

When you're one of the highest paid, highest profile people in your industry, you can effect a bigger change. You'll have more visibility to change the things in this world that matter to you. You'll have the money and resources to make a much bigger impact.

As William Penn, the founder of the province that later became the state of Pennsylvania said, "He that does good for good's sake seeks neither paradise nor reward, but he is sure of both in the end."

# RAPPORT: *Have Fulfilling Relationships*

The key to having fulfilling relationships is intent. You have to DECIDE that you'll have fulfilling relationships and then engage with the people in your life in ways that will allow the relationship to be fulfilling to you. And this doesn't go only for romantic or family relationships. We're talking about ALL of your relationships, from the very intimate to relationships with strangers.

You have to be selective in how you engage with the people you're in a relationship with. You need to treat your spouse differently than you treat your children. You need to engage differently with your sister than you do your co-workers. You even need to intentionally select how you engage with members of the public.

How do you present yourself in social media? We live in an interconnected Internet world and the things you post on Facebook, Twitter, or YouTube are likely to be seen by complete strangers. Leave the off color cartoons and jokes to those in the OTHER 98 percent.

How do you treat others when in public? Do you cut in front of others in line? Are you rude to waiters and cashiers? Do you demonstrate road rage? Of course YOU don't do these things, but you probably know people who do. What does that do to your opinion of them? Every person you meet should be considered a potential customer.

The key is understanding the individuals in the relationship. For family members, you need to accept their love and support in the way that they CHOOSE to give it, rather than in the way you want to receive it. If you're focusing on how they DO show their love, then you'll be fulfilled in the relationship. If you're expecting people to behave differently that they are, you'll be frustrated.

Thinking of the *Art of Selective Engagement*, you have the power to create the relationships with the people in your life. You can choose to have relationships with those who support and fulfill you, and you can pull back and be more selective with those who don't.

Our relationships with others have the ability to complete and fulfill us in a way that nothing else can. The key to having fulfilling relationships is the idea of deciding to do so, and selecting to engage with people in a way that allows the relationship to be fulfilling.

RAPPORT

# Rapport: *Negotiate and Make Great Deals*

People who are in the top 2 percent are the ones who know how to negotiate ETHICALLY. It's not about cheating someone or getting your way at all costs. Billionaire J.Paul Getty is quoted as saying, "My father said: 'You must never try to make all the money that's in a deal. Let the other fellow make some money too, because if you have a reputation for always making all the money, you won't have many deals.'"

# So, what are the steps in Collaborative Persuasion?

RAPPORT

THE TOP 2%

# Step One:

*Understanding the other person's viewpoint.* Other people's thinking and the filters they have are the source of the differences between the two of you. The magnitude of any problem has to do with the difference between their viewpoints and yours. When two people, or groups for that matter, have a conflict, they may be blaming the other person (or group) for something that happened. Most people think that you need to get at the objective truth of what happened. They do research and find facts and data to support their own viewpoints. But ultimately, conflict lies not in objective reality, but in people's minds. Discovering the facts may not solve the problem at all. Both parties might agree on the facts, but may still disagree on what should be done about the problem.

Here are some suggestions for understanding the other person's viewpoint. Words like, "Let me understand this from your perspective" can help. Repeat back what you've heard in your own words. "Okay, so correct me if I'm wrong, but what I'm hearing is…" and keep going back and forth until the person feels that you understand his or her point of view. You're not AGREEING with them, you're just understanding.

RAPPORT

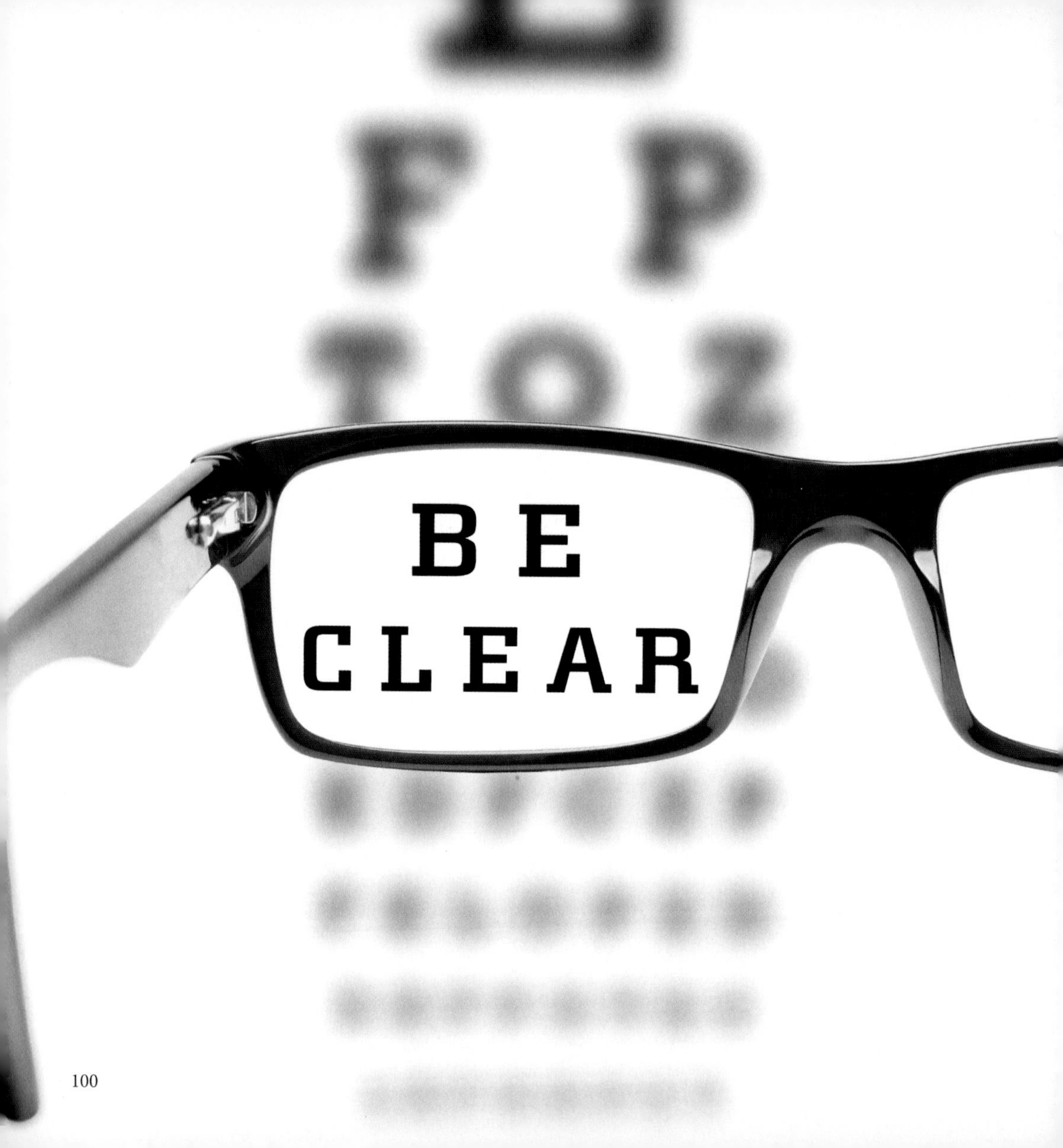
BE
CLEAR

# Step Two:

*Communicating your viewpoint.* To start, ask the other person if they are willing to hear your perspective. "Would you be willing to give me a fair hearing in return?" Then, explain how the other person's thoughts and feelings affect you. And make sure that you are clear that your perspective is YOUR experience, not the absolute truth. Ask the other person to repeat back what you just said. You can say, "Just so that we can be sure I expressed myself right, can you tell me how you heard what I just said?"

RAPPORT

# Step Three:

*Separating the positions from the problem.* This is a key step in negotiating. Here's a visual image that can represent what this step does. In traditional negotiation, you can imagine two people on opposite sides of a huge conference table. In the middle of the two is a piece of paper that represents the issue or the problem. Both people are trying to get the piece of paper to their own side of the table. "No, we're going to do it MY way."

In Collaborative Persuasion, you both come around to the same side of the table and focus on solving the problem! It's not about whose position is better or right. You have to separate that out

and identify the actual problem that needs to be solved. So you might say, "Okay, so you and I definitely see some things differently here. I see it this way, and your perception is this. But the fact is, we BOTH want to see this problem solved." You're inviting the other person to the other side of the table, so to speak, so that both of you can focus on solving the issue.

The ability to both see the situation from the other person's point of view and then to separate the positions from the problems is one of the most powerful negotiating skills you can possess.

**RAPPORT**

# Step Four:

*Jointly creating solutions.* Now it's time to brainstorm some solutions to the problem. Ask, "What ideas do you have to solve this problem?" If the solution that they come up with isn't acceptable to you for some reason, then you counter with a suggestion that is fair to both of you. If things start to get heated or emotional, as they often will, take a break. If the conversation starts to go back to positions and who is right and who is wrong, draw the attention back to the piece of paper in the middle of the table. It's about solving the problem, not being right. Don't be afraid of negative emotions but channel them to the solution instead of letting them derail the negotiation. Statements like, "I'm starting to feel frustrated right now. May we take a break?" or, "You seem to be getting angry. Do you need a break?" can go a long way to staying on the same side of the table.

*German billionaire Karl Albrecht, the man who was 11th on Forbes magazine's list of billionaires in 2011 might have been describing Collaborative Persuasion when he said, "Start out with an ideal and end with a deal."*

RAPPORT

# STARS

## SKILLS: *Goal Setting*

The final point of the star is the *Skills* that the highest paid, highest profile people in any industry have mastered.

The first of those four skills is *Goal Setting*. In order to become one of the highest paid, highest profile people in your industry, you need to set and MEET higher goals.

**To do that, we've developed a six-stage process called *Goal Scoping* that leads to the achievement of a goal:**

# Identify that a change needs to take place.

In *The Structure of Scientific Revolutions*, Thomas Kuhn says that change doesn't happen in a linear fashion. In other words, it's not just a steady improvement day after day. It's more like an explosive leap.

And that's how change happens. You're going along with the current state of thinking. This is the way things are. But pretty soon you start noticing anomalies and you're not so sure that you're right anymore. Soon, more and more anomalies are happening and you realize that the current paradigm is wrong. The status quo falls apart. This is a time of change—of confusion—of conflict. Then a bunch of competing theories about what's right pop up. Eventually one of them wins and becomes the new paradigm and everyone leaps into that new paradigm and it becomes the status quo; until anomalies start popping up again and the whole process starts again.

SKILLS

## Sufficient pain or displeasure with the current situation.

So, how bad is your current state, REALLY? You see, this is a key reason why people don't achieve their goals. The current situation isn't really bad enough. Sometimes people raise their tolerance for pain instead of eliminating the source of the pain. It's the old parable of how to cook a frog. You just turn the heat up slowly and the frog won't ever realize that it's being cooked. In life, we get progressively use to the status quo; until we start noticing anomalies that increase our awareness of the pain. The pain was always there, but you start noticing it more and more. And once it hits a threshold, you finally say, "No more."

SKILLS

### Identify what it will look like when the change has been made.

The end state. This is the place where you choose to think big or to be like the other 98 percent. Using a weight-loss example, maybe you decide that in addition to losing those holiday pounds, you want to get down to your college weight. You don't HAVE to set big, out-of-the-box, revolutionary goals. But, if you're looking to be one of the highest paid, highest profile people in your industry, you're going to need to think about what it would be like if you effected change on a large scale.

The clearer your vision for that end state is, the easier it will be for you to get there.

# Assurance that the new state will be better than the current state.

This is where things like visualization, affirmations, goal cards, and the other traditional goal-setting techniques can help. The more often you can remind yourself of how great the new situation will be, the easier the transition will become.

But here is an important distinction when you're creating a vision for the future. Author and speaker Mike Dooley says, "The details are visualized to get you excited about your end results, not to be your end results." In other words, it's not about creating the specific image in your mind that you're going to exactly have at the end.

When Steve Jobs developed the iPad, he had no idea what it was going to look like. In fact they developed another tablet computer early on that doesn't resemble the iPad at all. But I'll bet you anything, Steve Jobs had an image of SOME KIND of tablet computer. And he was able to FEEL how exciting such a device would be.

So, in stage four, you create a vision for the end state in order to get yourself to FEEL the feelings, rather than to nail down the details. This is what separates the top 2 percent from the rest. If you have a goal that's so outside the box that you can't even visualize it, don't worry. Just feel how great it will be to solve whatever problem your goal is trying to solve.

# Knowledge of the specific actions to take.
# You know what to do.

This is the easiest part of the whole process. No matter what you can think of, there is someone else on the planet that knows how to do it. You can learn from a role model or mentor, read books, listen to audio programs, take classes, or use some other way to learn pretty much anything you need to learn to get from where you are now to where you want to be.

Find both people who have already solved the problem you want to solve, and others who are in the same place you are.

## The belief that you can take those actions through self efficacy — your sense of competence.

You can achieve the goals that will rocket you to the top of your field. As Earl Nightingale said, "People with goals succeed because they know where they are going. It's as simple as that."

# SKILLS: *Time Management*

Whether you're the most successful person in your industry or a slacker, you still get 24 hours in a day. No more, no less. What makes the difference is how you spend your time. And how you spend your time depends on how you THINK about your time. The STARS actually think about the value of their time differently than everyone else.

We're not talking about someone with an arrogant attitude that, "my time is more valuable than yours." No, what we're talking about is the understanding that we only get 24 hours in a day and in order to make the best use of those hours you need to know what it is that you're good at and focus on doing those things, and either delegate or eliminate the things that aren't a good use of your time.

How can you learn to think about your time differently? We've developed a system called *Power Prioritization* that will allow you to shift your thinking about time and how you manage it.

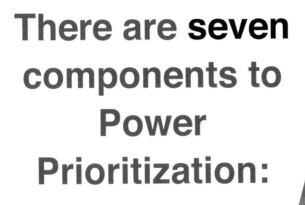

There are **seven** components to Power Prioritization:

SKILLS

THE TOP 2%

# Values: *The things that are important to you.*

Use your core personal values as your guide. What is important to you?

What are the things that matter to you?

# Goals: *What are the things you want to change or accomplish in your life?*

# Talents: *Your natural talents and abilities.*

What are the things you are naturally good at? What do you do best? A management consultant once told me, "It's better to maximize your natural talents and abilities so that you can spend your time doing those things instead of trying to get better at the things you don't do as well. Build your life around doing the things you're good at, and delegate or eliminate the things you don't do well.

# Desires: *Things you want to spend your time doing.*

What do you WANT to spend your time doing? Just because you're good at something doesn't mean you want to do it. Similarly, there might be things you LIKE doing that have no relationship to your values or talents.

## You: *Things that only you can do.*

There are some things that only YOU can do. Sometimes we use this as an excuse to get overcommitted or focus on the wrong things. A good question to ask is, "If I weren't here to do this, what would happen?" In many cases, the meeting would go on, the brownies would get baked, the job would get done. But there are a few things where you are the only one who can do it. It's your unique presence that defines success in this case. This is a really important distinction to make, because too often we spend our time on things that we THINK only we can do and don't focus on the unique gifts and talents we have to share.

**SKILLS**

**Others:** *Things that you need other people to help you accomplish.*

The sixth component of the Power Prioritization system is *Others*. There are some things that you may want to do, but can't do on your own. You need other people to participate. This is where the idea of leveraging your time comes into play. The highest paid, highest profile people understand that they can get more accomplished working with others than they can by themselves. Again, we've only got 24 hours in a day. If you want to accomplish great things, you're going to need to pool your 24 hours with other people.

# Basics: *The basic things you need to include in your life.*

These are the things that everyone needs to include in life like eating, sleeping, grooming, sex and exercise.

How do you apply the seven components of the Power Prioritization system to actually deciding how to manage your daily allotment of 24 hours?

After writing your goals, list everything that you want to include in your life on a daily or weekly basis. These should ideally be related to your goals and to the things you simply desire to do, as well as the basics that everyone needs to take care of.

Next, create a weekly template that is used for every week, scheduling in a time every day or every week to fit in each one of the things on your list.

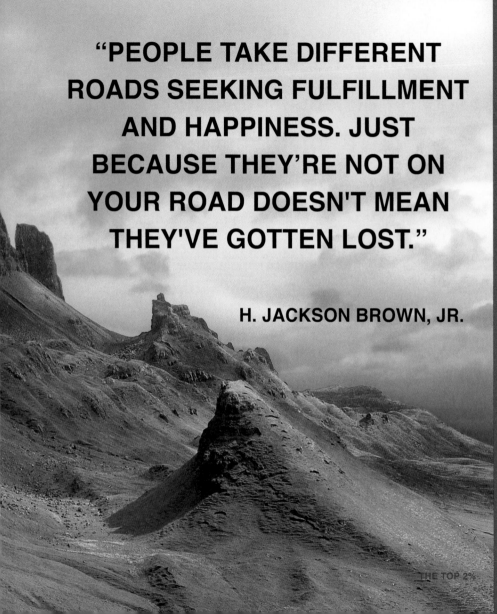

"PEOPLE TAKE DIFFERENT ROADS SEEKING FULFILLMENT AND HAPPINESS. JUST BECAUSE THEY'RE NOT ON YOUR ROAD DOESN'T MEAN THEY'VE GOTTEN LOST."

H. JACKSON BROWN, JR.

**It's not about WHAT you put in your schedule; it's about WHY you're doing what you do, and WHEN.**

The last part of the Power Prioritization System is to create a daily schedule based on the weekly template you just created. First thing every morning, or even better, the last thing you do at night, plan the day ahead. By doing this extra step, and not just trying to stick to the weekly template, you're allowing some flexibility.

Using the Power Prioritization System, you'll learn to leverage the 24 hours you are given each day to make the most of your life. That is how you think like the STARS.

TO DO LIST

1. Leverage your 24 hours _____

2. _____

3. _____

4. _____

5. _____

6. _____

SKILLS

# SKILLS: *Superior Money Management*

The principle of interval training, where you intersperse short bursts of intense energy with periods of lower intensity training, can also be applied to your wealth building. By doing so you'll build your wealth much, much faster than if you were to use another strategy.

*The first Interval is called Basic Money Skills.* Income and expenses need to balance out in Interval One. Develop a budget. It's just a fancy way of saying planning and tracking.

It's not about tackling credit card debt or even about saving money. It's about developing the core skills that you'll need to manage your wealth when you get it.

*Interval Two is the debt reduction phase.* Completely stop using credit cards, for anything, ever. And two, you're going to need to come up with some money for savings. Whether you pay yourself first, or do it after the credit card payments are gone, Interval Two is about getting rid of your debts and building up a little savings.

*Interval Three is where people tend to separate into levels.* Wealthy people THINK about money differently than non-wealthy people:

**MINDSET #1**. If you are being paid by the hour for your time, you're never going to be wealthy. It doesn't matter if you're the most highly paid hourly earner on the planet. You won't be truly wealthy because there is a limit to the amount of money you can make, and that limit is defined by time.

**SKILLS**

The way you build wealth is through the idea of leverage. You can leverage your money through people or through investments. Or both.

Albert Einstein once said that the most powerful force in the universe is compound interest. Why not use that force to your advantage? That's how you leverage money. An example of the power of leveraging people is the launch of a cookie dough business. When starting out, you are limited to the amount of cookie dough you could produce. But, by hiring more people to make the dough, you can create more profit.

This is the essence of wealth building; leveraging your money, or leveraging the time of other people. Ideally you'll do both.

**MINDSET #2**: Your wealth is directly related to the value of the service you provide to others. But it's not what YOU value; it's what OTHER people value.

The highest paid, highest profile people in every industry believe that they deserve to be wealthy. And they understand that their wealth is a gift that is to be used in service of something greater than themselves. Oprah and Madonna built schools for impoverished children. Bill Gates and his wife started a foundation. Each of these people has a different way of thinking about money. They see it as a spiritual energy that can be directed to solve a problem that is so big that no one person can solve it alone.

The legacy you leave is tied in to the wealth you have, which is tied in to the relationships you develop, which is affected by the way you manage time. All of the points on the STARS model are connected, and at the center of the star is your mindset. Earl Nightingale said it very succinctly when he said,

"The amount of money we receive will always be in direct ratio to the demand for what we do; our ability to do it; and the difficulty in replacing us."

**SKILLS**

THE TOP 2%

# SKILLS: *Creative Problem Solving*

Creative problem solving really is the foundational skill that supports your success in each of the other areas. If you're a creative thinker, you'll be able to overcome obstacles to your health, your finances, your relationships, and all of the other qualities on the STARS model.

The symbol of the monkey illustrates several important points about creativity and problem solving.

First, the monkey represents the attitude of curiosity. People who are creative problem solvers approach problems with an attitude of curiosity. "I wonder how we can solve this?" This is in stark contrast to the other 98 percent of people who see problems as obstacles or setbacks. Walt Disney said, "When you're curious, you find lots of interesting things to do."

So, how can you develop curiosity? Here are five ways you can train yourself to be curious.

# Ask why.

Develop an inquisitive attitude, broaden your perspectives.

# Ask how.

How does it happen? How do we proceed?

# Ask what if.

Speculate, imagine, visualize.

**Don't accept anything as a "fact."**

**Learn to be curious by always asking questions like why, how and what if.**

The next way that a monkey symbolizes creativity is through the concept of Monkey Mind—the presence of thoughts that keep jumping around and disturbing you. Now, typically in meditation or yoga, Monkey Mind is

**SKILLS**

considered a bad thing. And if you're trying to empty your mind, it is. But as a creative problem–solving technique, it can be very useful. The Monkey Mind Map can be a brainstorming exercise that helps you to use that creative monkey mind to help you solve a problem. Here's how it works. Calm your mind by taking a few deep breaths and center yourself.

On a piece of paper, write down a word that represents the problem or block you're facing. Then, look at that word and let your monkey mind think of everything to do with that problem. Write down those words. Then, look at each of those words and see what comes to mind. Not every word will lead somewhere, but some might. If you come up against a block, ask the Monkey Mind a direct question. "What is another way of looking at this?" Then wait and see what the Monkey Mind says.

You might not hit on a solution right away. You might need to put the Monkey Mind Map aside and think of something else for awhile. But soon you'll have a dream or a thought or an idea and it will be a creative solution to your problem.

SKILLS

"WHAT YOU GET BY ACHIEVING YOUR GOALS IS NOT AS IMPORTANT AS WHAT YOU BECOME BY ACHIEVING YOUR GOALS."

HENRY DAVID THOREAU

# Conclusion

With the entire STARS model, you have learned the traits, attributes, rapport qualities, and skills of the highest paid, highest profile people in every industry. And you've learned how to connect it all to an overarching sense of purpose.

Now you're on your way to becoming one of the highest paid, highest profile people in YOUR industry.

As Earl Nightingale said, "We can help others in the world more by making the most of yourself than in any other way."

Using these skills, the quality of your life will be measurably better than it is today.

This is your life, and these are your dreams. This is a unique opportunity to take the steps to improve every aspect of your life. Enjoy the journey.

# THE TOP 2%

**S**ense of Purpose

**T**raits

**A**ttributes

**R**apport with others

**S**kills

# How close are you from entering the exclusive world of money, power, health, and charity?

Learn what those in the Top 2% have learned, do what they do and **YOU** can join their ranks.

No matter what you might think or have been taught, getting what you want out of life isn't about IQ, education or luck. It's about mastering a specific, unique set of skills, mind sets, and habits.

## 2 minutes. 28 days. Lifelong results.

Using just 2 MINUTES of your day for 28 DAYS, you will begin to see DRAMATIC improvements in your finances, career, relationships, and health.

**TODAY Begin Your 28 Day Challenge!**

**Log on today!**

## Start the 28-Day Challenge Today, *visit us at:*

# www.StartThe28DayChallenge.com

Nightingale-Conant 1400 S. Wolf Rd., Building 300, Suite 103, Wheeling, Il 60090

If you have enjoyed this book we invite you to check out our entire collection of gift books, with free inspirational movies, at www.simpletruths.com. You'll discover it's a great way to inspire friends and family, or to thank your best customers and employees.